SECRET GUIDE TO 2X *Profits* FOR COSMETICS SHOPS

SECRET GUIDE TO 2X *Profits* FOR COSMETICS SHOPS

Ashish Gupta

Worldwide Published by
Pendown Press

PENDOWN PRESS LLP

An ISO 9001 & ISO 14001 Certified Co.,

Regd. Office: 3767A, Kanhaiya Nagar,

Tri Nagar, Delhi-110035

Ph.: 8130886000, 9650072927

E-mail: info@pendownpress.com

Branch Office: 1A/2A, 20, Hari Sadan, Ansari Road,

Daryaganj, New Delhi-110002

Ph.: 011-45794768

Website: PendownPress.com

Edition: 2024

Price: ₹ 299

ISBN: 978-93-6338-299-2

Layout and Cover Designed by Pendown Graphics Team

Printed and Bound in India by Thomson Press India Ltd.

To all the dedicated cosmetic shop owners,

This book is for you—the passionate individuals who bring beauty and joy to every customer. Your hard work and commitment make a real difference in people's lives.

Thank you for all the effort you put in, day in and day out.

Contents

Preface	ii
Do You know	iv
Acknowledgements	vi
Why This Book?	vii
Chapter 1	**01**
Cosmetics in the Digital Era	
Chapter 2	**07**
Online Competition: A Makeup of Problems for Retailers	
Chapter 3	**14**
Three Core Strategies for Business Growth	
Chapter 4	**21**
High-Profit Formula	
Chapter 5	**28**
Why Originals Only?	
Chapter 6	**34**
Make the Most of Company Offers	
Chapter 7	**39**
Mastering the Art of Selling	
Chapter 8	**44**
Direct Communication Tools for Your Cosmetic Shops	
Let's Conquer the Cosmetic Market	**49**

Preface

Is your cosmetic shop thriving or just surviving?

It's time to turn the table. This book is your roadmap to transforming your business from ordinary to extraordinary.

Imagine a shop where customers are not just visitors but valued guests. Where every product tells a story, and every interaction builds a lasting relationship. This book will show you how to create that kind of magic.

The book is designed to be your guide, offering straightforward strategies, real-life case studies, and insights to help you excel in the ever-evolving cosmetic industry. From mastering customer relationships to optimizing inventory and embracing the latest selling techniques, this book covers essential topics that will help you navigate the challenges and seize the opportunities in your business.

You'll learn how to create a captivating store environment that draws customers in and keeps them coming back. Discover the power of digital marketing and how to leverage social media to your advantage. Master the art of customer service and build a loyal customer base that will become your greatest advocates.

But it's not just about sales; it's about creating an experience. Learn how to position your shop as a destination, a place where customers can discover new products, indulge in self-care, and feel inspired. By understanding the psychology behind consumer behavior, you can tailor your offerings to meet their desires and exceed their expectations.

So, if you're ready to take your business to new heights and make a lasting impact in the world of cosmetics, let's do this! Thanks for joining me on this journey, and we can't wait to see the amazing things you'll achieve!

■ ■ ■ ■

Do You know?

India's beauty and personal care market is set to explode, reaching a whopping $30 billion by 2027.

[**Source:** Report launched by Redseer Strategy Consultants along with Peak XV]

Are you ready to make your mark?

Don't miss this golden opportunity. I know how it feels to be passionate about making people feel confident and beautiful. I've been in your shoes, working tirelessly to create a welcoming space that makes customers feel like they're part of something special.

But let's be real - running a cosmetic shop can be tough! From keeping up with trends to managing inventory, it's easy to get overwhelmed. That's why I wrote this book - to share my own experiences, successes, and failures with you.

Inside these pages, I'll share practical tips and real-life stories to help you:

- Create a store that feels like a warm hug to your customers

- Build relationships that keep them coming back for more
- Stay ahead of the curve without breaking the bank
- And so much more!

Don't let your cosmetic shop struggle any longer. Get the solutions you need to succeed and start building the business of your dreams today!

■ ■ ■ ■

Acknowledgements

Dear Readers,

I am grateful for the opportunity to share my experiences and insights with you. This book represents a compilation of years of experience, learning, and growth. I hope that the words within these pages inspire, inform, and resonate with each reader.

I am deeply grateful to the wonderful individuals who have played instrumental roles in shaping my journey and contributing to my achievements.

My mentor, Akshar Yadav Sir (aka My Krishna), your guidance and wisdom have shaped me into the person I am today. I owe much of my success to your invaluable mentorship.

To all those not named, your contributions have been crucial to my journey. Together, we have built something extraordinary, and I look forward to continuing this journey of growth and success with each one of you.

Thank you for being a part of this shared experience.

■ ■ ■ ■

Why This Book?

Are you tired of:

- Throwing money at marketing strategies that don't work?
- Watching customers walk out of your store without making a purchase?
- Feeling like you're constantly playing catch-up with the latest trends and products?
- Struggling to build a loyal customer base that will drive sales and growth?

You're not alone. Many cosmetic shop owners face these same challenges every day. But what if you could:

- Attract and retain customers who love your brand and can't wait to come back?
- Drive sales and revenue without breaking the bank?
- Stay ahead of the curve and make informed decisions about products and trends?
- Build a thriving business that brings you joy and financial freedom?

This book is the solution you've been searching for. With its practical advice and real-life examples, you'll learn how to:

- Create a welcoming store environment that makes customers feel like royalty
- Build relationships that keep customers coming back for more
- Stay ahead of the curve without breaking the bank
- Drive sales and revenue through proven strategies and techniques

So, grab a cup of coffee and let's get started!

■ ■ ■ ■

Chapter 1

Cosmetics in the Digital Era

"Technology alone is not enough." – Steve Jobs

The Impact of Online Shopping on Traditional Cosmetic Shops

The rise of online shopping has undoubtedly shaken up the traditional cosmetic retail landscape. For many small business owners, this shift has led to decreased sales and increased competition. This shift necessitates understanding the dynamics of the change and finding ways to adapt to stay competitive in the market. In this detailed analysis, we will explore how online shopping has impacted traditional cosmetic shops, the reasons behind this trend, and potential strategies to counteract the decline in sales.

The Rise of Online Shopping

Over the last decade, online shopping has transformed the way consumers purchase goods, including cosmetics. E-commerce platforms like Amazon, Flipkart, Nykaa, and others have made it convenient for consumers to browse and buy products from the comfort of their homes. The ease of access, wide variety of products, competitive pricing, and frequent discounts offered by these platforms have made online shopping a preferred choice for many. Several factors have contributed to this rapid growth:

- **Convenience and Accessibility:** Online shopping offers the convenience of 24/7 availability, price comparisons, reviews, and easy decision-making without leaving home.
- **Wider Product Range:** E-commerce platforms can stock a vast array of products, unlike physical stores limited by shelf space, attracting customers seeking specific or niche products.
- **Competitive Pricing and Discounts:** Online retailers often have lower operational costs, allowing them to offer lower prices and frequent discounts, challenging traditional shops with higher overhead costs.
- **Consumer Reviews and Ratings:** Online platforms provide reviews and ratings, helping customers make informed decisions, a feature that traditional shops lack.

Major Differences B/W

Retail Shops	Online ki Duniya
Personalized Service: Face-to-face interaction allows for personalized recommendations and a human touch.	**Lack of Personal Interaction:** No face-to-face customer service can lead to a less personal shopping experience.
Immediate Product Availability: Customers can see, touch, and try products before purchasing.	**Delayed Gratification:** Products need to be shipped, causing delays in receiving items.
Community Engagement: Builds local community ties and supports the local economy.	**Impersonal Transactions:** Transactions lack the personal touch and community engagement.
Trust and Loyalty: Long-standing relationships with customers foster trust and loyalty.	**Risk of Fraud:** Higher chances of encountering counterfeit products or fraudulent sellers.
In-Store Events: Opportunities for live product demonstrations, beauty consultations, and sampling.	**No Physical Experience:** Customers cannot physically interact with products before buying.
Immediate Problem Resolution: Issues can be addressed on the spot, providing instant customer satisfaction.	**Difficult Returns:** Returns and exchanges can be complicated and time-consuming.

Impact on Sales of Traditional Cosmetic Shops

The convenience, variety, competitive pricing, and review availability of online shopping have led to a preference for online purchases, resulting in reduced sales for traditional shops. Many small and medium-sized businesses have been hit particularly hard, struggling to keep up with the pace of change. This decline in foot traffic and sales has prompted traditional cosmetic shops to seek new strategies to attract and retain customers.

Strategies for Traditional Cosmetic Shops to Adapt

Despite the challenges posed by online shopping, traditional cosmetic shops can adopt several strategies to stay competitive and attract customers. Here are some effective approaches:

1. **Enhancing In-Store Experience:**
    - The physical store should become a destination. Offer personalized consultations, expert advice, and interactive experiences that can't be replicated online
    - Consider hosting makeup workshops, skincare consultations, or even mini-spa treatments
2. **Leveraging Social Media:**
    - Using platforms like Instagram, Facebook, and YouTube to showcase products and interact with customers
    - Sharing engaging content such as tutorials, reviews, and behind-the-scenes looks

3. **Offering Loyalty Programs:**
   - Implementing programs that reward customers for purchases, referrals, or social media engagement
   - Providing exclusive discounts, special offers, and members-only events
4. **Focusing on Local Community:**
   - Collaborating with local influencers and participating in community events
   - Supporting local causes to enhance reputation and attract local customers
5. **Providing Exceptional Customer Service:**
   - Training staff on product knowledge, customer interaction, and problem-solving
   - Ensuring a positive customer experience to build trust and loyalty

We will discuss these points in more detail in the upcoming chapters.

Key Takeaways

Online sales have reduced the revenue for traditional cosmetic shop retailers.

Conclusion

The rise of online shopping has undoubtedly posed challenges for traditional cosmetic shop retailers. However, by understanding the reasons behind this trend and implementing strategic changes, traditional shops can remain competitive.

Enhancing the in-store experience, building an online presence, leveraging social media, offering loyalty programs, focusing on the local community, and providing exceptional customer service are all effective strategies to attract and retain customers. Adapting to the evolving market landscape is crucial for the survival and growth of traditional cosmetic shops in the digital age.

Chapter 2

Online Competition: A Makeup of Problems for Retailers

"Arise, awake, and stop not till the goal is reached." – Swami Vivekananda

Problems Faced by Cosmetic Retailers Due to Online Business

As we discussed, the rise of online shopping has posed significant challenges to traditional cosmetic retailers. These challenges include reducing profit margins, decreasing sales, losing customers, diminished motivation for the next generation to enter the business, and uncertainty about how to move forward. This detailed chapter aims to explain these problems in easy-to-understand language and provide insights for cosmetic shop owners on how to address these issues.

1. Reducing Profit Margins

One of the most significant problems faced by traditional cosmetic retailers due to the rise of online businesses is the reduction in profit margins. Several factors contribute to this issue:

- **Competitive Pricing:** Online retailers often operate with lower overhead costs compared to brick-and-mortar stores. They save on rent, utilities, and in-store staffing, allowing them to offer products at lower prices. This makes it difficult for traditional retailers to compete, as they have higher fixed costs and less flexibility to reduce prices without affecting their profit margins.
- **Frequent Discounts and Promotions:** Online platforms frequently offer discounts, sales, and promotional deals to attract customers. These promotions can include seasonal sales, flash sales, and special discounts for members. Traditional stores may find it challenging to match these offers, leading to a further reduction in their profit margins as they try to stay competitive.
- **Bulk Buying and Economy of Scale:** Large online retailers often purchase products in bulk, benefiting from economies of scale. This means they can negotiate better prices with suppliers, reducing their costs per unit. Traditional cosmetic shops, especially smaller ones, may not have the purchasing power to negotiate similar deals, putting them at a disadvantage.

2. **Decreasing Sales**

The shift to online shopping has led to a noticeable decrease in sales for many traditional cosmetic retailers. Several factors contribute to this decline:

- **Convenience of Online Shopping:** One of the main reasons consumers prefer online shopping is the convenience it offers. Customers can shop from the comfort of their homes, avoiding the need to travel to a physical store. Online shopping is available 24/7, allowing consumers to make purchases at any time that suits them. This convenience is a significant draw, leading to reduced foot traffic in traditional stores.
- **Wider Product Range:** Online platforms can offer a vast array of products that might not be available in a single physical store. This variety attracts customers who are looking for specific or niche products that might be hard to find in local shops. Traditional cosmetic retailers often have limited shelf space and may not be able to stock every brand or product variant, leading to a loss of customers seeking more options.
- **Customer Reviews and Ratings:** Online shopping platforms provide consumers with access to reviews and ratings from other buyers. This feature helps customers make informed decisions based on the experiences of others. Traditional shops lack this real-time feedback mechanism, making it harder for consumers to gauge the quality and effectiveness of a product before purchase. The trust built through positive reviews online often drives customers away from physical stores.

3. Losing Customers

The combination of competitive pricing, convenience, and wider product range offered by online retailers has resulted in traditional cosmetic shops losing customers. This loss can be attributed to several factors:

- **Price Sensitivity:** Price-sensitive customers are more likely to switch to online platforms where they can find better deals and discounts. Traditional stores, with their higher overhead costs, find it challenging to match these prices, leading to a loss of price-sensitive customers.
- **Lack of Product Availability:** Customers seeking specific products that are not available in traditional stores are more likely to turn to online platforms. This is especially true for niche or less common items that local shops may not stock. As a result, traditional retailers lose customers to online stores that can meet their specific needs.
- **Evolving Consumer Behavior:** Consumer behavior has evolved with the rise of technology and the internet. Younger generations, in particular, are more comfortable with online shopping and prefer the convenience it offers. Traditional retailers may struggle to attract and retain these tech-savvy customers, leading to a gradual decline in their customer base.

4. Diminished Motivation for the Next Generation

The challenges faced by traditional cosmetic retailers have also led to diminished motivation for the next generation to enter the business. This issue is multifaceted:

- **Perception of a Declining Industry:** The visible struggles of traditional stores, such as decreasing sales and reduced profit margins, can create a perception that the industry is in decline. This perception can discourage the next generation from considering a career in the family business or starting their own cosmetic retail shop.
- **Lack of Opportunities:** With the rise of online shopping, many young entrepreneurs see more opportunities in the digital space rather than in traditional retail. They may prefer to start an online business, where they can leverage technology and reach a broader audience, rather than investing in a brick-and-mortar store.
- **Financial Uncertainty:** The financial challenges faced by traditional retailers, including high operational costs and competitive pressure from online platforms, can create an uncertain financial future. This uncertainty can deter the next generation from taking on the risks associated with running a traditional cosmetic shop.

5. Uncertainty About the Future

The rapidly changing retail landscape has left many traditional cosmetic shop owners uncertain about the future and unsure of what steps to take to remain competitive. This uncertainty can stem from several factors:

- **Lack of Digital Skills:** Many traditional retailers lack the digital skills needed to compete in the online world. This includes skills related to e-commerce, digital marketing, and social media. Without these skills, it can be challenging to establish an online presence and attract customers.
- **Fear of Change:** Change can be daunting, especially for long-established businesses. The shift to online retail requires a willingness to adapt and embrace new technologies and strategies. However, fear of change and the unknown can prevent traditional shop owners from taking the necessary steps to stay competitive.
- **Need for Investment:** Establishing an online presence and implementing new strategies often require investment in technology, training, and marketing. Traditional retailers may be hesitant to make these investments, especially if they are unsure of the potential returns.
- **Strategies to Address These Challenges:** While the challenges faced by traditional cosmetic retailers are significant, there are several strategies that can help address these issues and ensure continued success:
- **Embrace Omnichannel Retailing:** Combining online and offline retail strategies can help traditional shops compete more effectively. This approach, known as

omnichannel retailing, allows customers to shop in a way that suits them best, whether online or in-store. Implementing click-and-collect services, where customers can order online and pick up in-store, can also bridge the gap between digital and physical shopping.

- **Invest in Digital Skills:** Traditional retailers should invest in developing digital skills, either through training or hiring experts. Understanding e-commerce, digital marketing, and social media can help establish a strong online presence and attract new customers.

Key Takeaways

Problems Faced by Cosmetic Retailers Due to Online Business: Reducing profit, declining sales, shrinking customer base, lack of motivation due to the next generation not joining the business, and insufficient knowledge on how to address these challenges.

Conclusion

To wrap up, the growth of online shopping has brought serious challenges for traditional cosmetic stores. These include lower profits, fewer sales, and a shrinking customer base. The rise of online shopping has also made younger people less interested in joining the business and left many store owners unsure of what to do next. To tackle these issues, cosmetic retailers should blend online and in-store sales and improve their digital skills to stay competitive.

Chapter 3

Three Core Strategies for Business Growth

"Your most unhappy customers are your greatest source of learning." – Bill Gates

What We Can Do: Three Broad Steps to Revitalize Our Cosmetic Shops

Running a successful cosmetic shop has always relied on some key principles. But in the rush of daily business, it's easy to forget these basics. By going back to these core steps, we can refresh our stores, draw in more customers, and stay competitive with online sellers. Here, we'll look at three important strategies that we've learned over the years but might have overlooked because of our busy lives.

Three Core Strategies to Revitalize Our Cosmetic Shops

1. **Customer Relationships: Building and Maintaining Trust**

Building strong customer relationships is the backbone of any successful business. This is especially true for cosmetic shops, where personalized service and trust play a crucial role in customer satisfaction and loyalty.

Building and maintaining strong customer relationships is essential for success in the cosmetics industry. To foster trust, ensure consistent product quality and transparent communication about ingredients, pricing, and policies. Personalize service by remembering customer preferences and offering tailored recommendations. Honest marketing and addressing issues promptly are crucial for credibility. Regular engagement through follow-ups and loyalty programs helps keep customers connected and informed. Infuse a human touch by providing warm, empathetic service and actively listening to customer feedback. Additionally, invest in staff training to enhance service quality and create a welcoming store atmosphere. By focusing on these aspects, you build lasting trust and loyalty, leading to stronger customer relationships and sustained business success.

2. **In-Store Experience: Making Shopping Enjoyable and Memorable**

Creating an enjoyable and memorable in-store experience is another critical step. While online shopping is convenient, it lacks the sensory experience that a physical store can provide. By focusing on the in-store experience, you can attract and retain more customers.

Store Layout and Ambiance

The layout and ambiance of your store can significantly impact the customer experience. Here are some tips to enhance your store's atmosphere:

- **Clean and Organized:** Keep your store clean and well-organized. Ensure that products are neatly arranged and easy to find. An organized store makes for a pleasant shopping experience and encourages customers to spend more time browsing.
- **Lighting and Decor:** Use lighting and decor to create a welcoming and relaxing environment. Soft lighting can make the store feel cozy, while strategic use of mirrors and displays can make the space feel larger and more inviting.
- **Music and Scents:** Consider playing soft background music and using pleasant scents to enhance the sensory experience. However, make sure that these elements are not overwhelming and complement the overall ambiance.

Interactive Elements

Adding interactive elements to your store can make the shopping experience more engaging and enjoyable:

- **Product Demonstrations:** Host regular product demonstrations and tutorials. This allows customers to see how products work and ask questions in real time. It also provides an opportunity to showcase the benefits of new or popular items.
- **Sampling Stations:** Set up sampling stations where customers can try out products before buying. This is

particularly effective for cosmetics, as customers often want to see how a product looks and feels on their skin.

- **Events and Workshops:** Organize beauty events and workshops, such as makeup classes or skincare consultations. These events can attract new customers and provide valuable information that enhances the shopping experience.

3. **Marketing and Community Engagement: Reaching and Retaining Customers**

Effective marketing and community engagement are essential for attracting new customers and retaining existing ones. While digital marketing is crucial in today's world, traditional marketing methods and community involvement should not be overlooked.

Digital Marketing

Digital marketing is crucial for strengthening customer relationships in the cosmetics industry. It boosts your shop's visibility through SEO and social media, allowing you to reach targeted audiences with personalized ads. Engaging customers via social media, sharing valuable content, and using email marketing keeps them informed and connected. Collecting feedback and analyzing data help you understand and meet customer needs. By integrating digital marketing, you enhance visibility, improve engagement, and build stronger relationships with your customers.

Traditional Marketing

While digital marketing is essential, traditional marketing methods can also be effective:

- **Flyers and Posters:** Distribute flyers and posters in your local area to promote special offers, new products, and upcoming events. Place them in high-traffic areas like community centers, libraries, and cafes.
- **Local Advertising:** Advertise in local newspapers, magazines, and radio stations. These channels can help you reach a local audience and build brand recognition in your community.
- **Collaborations:** Partner with other local businesses to cross-promote each other's products and services. This can help you reach new customers and build a network of support within your community.

Community Engagement

Engaging with your local community can build strong relationships and enhance your reputation:

- **Local Events:** Participate in local events, such as fairs, festivals, and charity fundraisers. Setting up a booth or sponsoring an event can increase your visibility and attract new customers.
- **Workshops and Seminars:** Host educational workshops and seminars on beauty and skincare topics. This provides value to your community and positions your

store as a knowledgeable and trustworthy source of information.

- **Customer Appreciation:** Show appreciation for your loyal customers through special events, discounts, and personalized thank-you notes. Recognizing and rewarding your customers can foster loyalty and encourage repeat business.

Key Takeaways

What we can do is expanded in the three broad steps above. Although we have known these strategies for years through practice and experience, we may have forgotten them due to our busy schedules.

Conclusion

In conclusion, by refocusing on these three broad steps – building and maintaining customer relationships, creating an enjoyable and memorable in-store experience, and implementing effective marketing and community engagement strategies – traditional cosmetic shops can thrive despite the challenges posed by online retailers. These practices, which we all know from years of experience, can help us attract more customers, increase sales, and build a loyal customer base. While the business landscape is changing, the core principles of customer service, experience, and engagement remain as important as ever. By remembering and implementing these steps, we can ensure the continued success of our cosmetic shops.

Case Study of Glam Garden

Anjali's cosmetic shop 'Glam Garden' is one of the city's most beloved stores. Every customer feels special here. Anjali believes that customers are not just sales figures but a part of a relationship.

Anjali has inspired her staff to know each customer personally. They remember customers' birthdays, weddings, or special occasions. Once, a regular customer, Juhi, was getting married. Anjali not only gifted her a makeup kit for the wedding but also helped with all the wedding preparations. These small efforts have earned Glam Garden a special place in the hearts of customers.

Anjali is also active on social media. She shares customers' photos, pays attention to their suggestions, and engages with them. This has not only increased the brand's reach but also strengthened the bond with customers.

Anjali believes that trust and relationships are the foundation of any business. Once a customer connects with you, they will always come back.

Chapter 4

High-Profit Formula

"Don't be afraid to give up the good to go for the great." – John D. Rockefeller

High Profit Formula

High-frequency products have low profit margins, whereas high-profit products have low demand but higher profits. Therefore, promote high-profit products more to increase your earnings.

Running a successful cosmetic shop involves not only stocking the right products but also effectively promoting them to maximize profits. One of the common challenges faced by shop owners is balancing the promotion of high-frequency low-margin products with high-profit low-demand items. While high-frequency products bring in steady sales, they often have lower profit margins. On the other hand, high-profit products can significantly boost your earnings but may not sell as quickly. This chapter will explore strategies to effectively promote high-profit products to increase your overall profitability while maintaining a healthy balance in your inventory.

Think of it like this

Running a makeup shop isn't just about having lots of products. You also need to know how to sell them to make money. There are two kinds of products:

1. **Everyday items:** These are things people buy often, like lipstick or mascara. They make you steady money but not a lot on each sale.
2. **High-end items:** These are special products like fancy skincare or expensive perfumes. They make you more money per sale but people don't buy them as often.

The trick is to sell both kinds to make the most money. You want to keep people coming back for the everyday stuff, but you also want to convince them to buy the more expensive things. This guide will help you do just that.

Understanding Product Categories

To effectively promote your products, it's essential to understand the two categories and their characteristics:

High-Frequency Low-Margin Products

- **Examples:** Basic skincare items, everyday makeup products, popular shampoos, and conditioners.
- **Characteristics:** These products sell quickly and are in constant demand. They attract a large number of customers but generate a lower profit per unit.
- **Importance:** They drive foot traffic and ensure regular sales, contributing to a steady cash flow.

High-Profit Low-Demand Products

- **Examples:** Premium skincare items, luxury cosmetics, niche fragrances, and high-end beauty gadgets.
- **Characteristics:** These products have higher profit margins but sell more slowly. They attract a smaller, more specific customer base.
- **Importance:** They can significantly increase your overall profitability when sold, adding substantial value per transaction.

Similarly, there are a few brands that take a low margin but have high demand due to their advertisements on TV, social media, and other marketing channels. On the other hand, there are brands that don't advertise but offer good margins to retailers.

Strategies for Promoting High-Profit Products

To maximize your earnings, it's crucial to effectively promote high-profit products without neglecting your high-frequency items. Here are several strategies to achieve this balance:

1. Educate Your Customers

To educate your customers about high-profit products, focus on providing comprehensive and engaging content through digital platforms. Utilize your social media channels to share informative articles, blog posts, and videos that highlight the benefits and unique features of these products.

Offer virtual consultations where customers can receive personalized advice and recommendations. Create an FAQ section addressing common questions and concerns about high-end items. By leveraging digital communication and providing valuable information, you can effectively educate customers and increase their interest in high-profit products.

2. **Create Attractive Displays**

Creating attractive displays is essential for drawing attention to high-profit products in your cosmetic shop. Use eye-catching designs and strategic placement to make these items stand out. Incorporate vibrant colors, proper lighting, and themed setups to highlight the luxury and exclusivity of high-end products. Placing these displays in prominent areas, such as near the entrance or at eye level, can entice customers to explore them further. By investing in visually appealing displays, you can enhance the perceived value of high-profit items and boost sales.

3. **Optimize Inventory Management**

Optimizing inventory management is crucial for maintaining a profitable cosmetic shop. Implement an efficient tracking system to monitor stock levels, sales trends, and product performance. Regularly analyze this data to identify which items are in high demand and which are underperforming. Adjust your orders accordingly to ensure you have sufficient stock of popular products while minimizing excess inventory of slower-selling items. By staying organized and proactive with inventory management, you can reduce costs, prevent stockouts, and ensure your shop is always ready to meet customer needs.

Managing Inventory Digitally

Imagine trying to keep track of all your makeup products without a system. It would be a total mess, right? That's where digital inventory management comes in.

Here's how it works:

- **Use software:** Use tools like Shopify, Vend, or Zoho Inventory to automate tracking, manage stock levels, and generate real-time reports. These platforms offer features such as automatic stock updates, reorder alerts, and integration with e-commerce channels.
- **Scan products:** You can use barcode scanners or even your smartphone to quickly count items.
- **Track sales:** The software automatically updates your inventory whenever you sell something.
- **Know what you need:** It tells you when you're running low on a product, so you can order more.
- **Save time and money:** By knowing exactly what you have, you avoid overstocking or running out of popular items.

Basically, it's like having a super smart assistant that helps you manage your makeup stash without the hassle.

Key Takeaways

High-frequency products have low profit margins, while high-profit products have lower demand but higher profit margins. To increase your earnings, focus on promoting more high-profit products to boost your revenue.

Conclusion

Balancing the promotion of high-frequency low-margin products with high-profit low-demand items is crucial for maximizing profitability in your cosmetic shop. By educating your customers, creating attractive displays, offering incentives, leveraging digital marketing, providing exceptional customer service, and optimizing inventory management, you can effectively promote high-profit products and increase your overall earnings.

Remember, the key to success lies in understanding your customers' needs and preferences, and strategically showcasing the value of high-profit items. With the right approach, you can achieve a healthy balance in your inventory and ensure a steady stream of revenue for your cosmetic shop. While high-frequency products bring in regular sales, high-profit products can significantly boost your profits, leading to more money in the bank and a thriving business.

Case Study of Mrs. Annu

Mrs. Annu opened a small cosmetic shop in her town. Initially, she focused on fast-selling products like lipsticks, eyeliners, and nail polishes. These products consistently brought in sales, but their profit margins were low. Over time, Annu realized that relying solely on these products was not enough to grow her business.

She decided to include high-profit products like anti-aging creams, serums, and high-end brands. However, these products were not selling quickly. Annu faced a challenge - how to sell these high-profit products without affecting the regular sales.

Anna devised a strategy. She divided her shop into two sections - one for fast-selling products and the other for high-profit products. She set up a special display for the high-profit products to catch customers' attention. Additionally, Anna trained her staff to provide detailed information about these products. The staff learned how to effectively communicate the benefits of the products to customers. Anna introduced activities like product demos, customer consultations, and loyalty programs.

As a result of these efforts, the sales of high-profit products in Annu's shop increased. Regular sales were not affected either. Annu found that it was essential to promote both types of products in a balanced way.

Today, Annu's shop is a successful business. She has proven that selling high-profit products can be challenging, but it can be achieved with the right strategy.

Chapter 5

Why Originals Only?

"You don't build a business. You build people, and people build the business." – Zig Ziglar

The Importance of Buying and Selling Only Original Products in Your Cosmetic Shop

In the competitive world of cosmetic retail, maintaining a reputation for quality and trustworthiness is crucial. One of the most important ways to ensure this is by only buying and selling original products. While it may be tempting to purchase cheaper, duplicate products to increase profit margins, this practice can have serious negative consequences for your business. In this chapter, we will explore the importance of buying original products, the risks associated with selling duplicates, and how to ensure you are sourcing and selling genuine items.

1. Why Original Products Matter

Quality and Safety

Original cosmetic products are manufactured under strict quality control standards. They contain ingredients that have been tested for safety and efficacy. Using these products, customers can trust that they are getting high-quality items that will not harm their skin or health. On the other hand, duplicate products often contain substandard or harmful ingredients that can cause allergic reactions, skin irritation, or more severe health issues.

- **Tested Ingredients:** Original products use ingredients that have been rigorously tested for safety. They comply with health and safety regulations and have been approved by relevant authorities.
- **Consistent Results:** Customers can rely on original products to deliver consistent results. Whether it's a foundation that matches their skin tone perfectly or a moisturizer that keeps their skin hydrated, genuine products perform as expected.

Brand Reputation

Selling original products helps maintain and enhance your shop's reputation. Customers trust well-known brands for their quality and effectiveness. By stocking original products, you align your store with these trusted brands, which can enhance your credibility and attract more customers.

- **Customer Trust:** Customers are more likely to trust and frequent a store that sells original products. Trust leads to repeat business and word-of-mouth recommendations.

- **Brand Partnerships:** Selling genuine products can open doors to partnerships with reputable brands. These partnerships can lead to exclusive product launches, special promotions, and other benefits.

2. **Risks of Selling Duplicate Products**

Legal Issues

Selling counterfeit products can lead to serious legal consequences. Brands invest significant resources in protecting their intellectual property. If you are caught selling fake products, you could face lawsuits, hefty fines, and even criminal charges.

- **Lawsuits:** Brands can sue for damages if you are found selling counterfeit versions of their products. These lawsuits can be costly and damaging to your business.
- **Fines and Penalties:** Regulatory authorities impose fines and penalties on businesses that sell counterfeit products. These fines can be substantial and harm your financial stability.

Damage to Reputation

Once customers realize that you are selling fake products, your reputation will suffer. Customers who have a bad experience with counterfeit products will likely share their negative experiences, leading to a loss of trust and a decline in business.

- **Customer Complaints:** Customers who experience adverse reactions or are dissatisfied with the performance of counterfeit products will complain, both directly to your store and online.
- **Negative Reviews:** Negative reviews on social media and review sites can deter potential customers from visiting your store. Reputation damage can be long-lasting and challenging to repair.

Health Risks

Duplicate cosmetic products often contain harmful ingredients that can cause serious health issues. Customers who experience these adverse effects will not only stop shopping at your store but may also take legal action against you.

- **Allergic Reactions:** Counterfeit products can contain allergens that cause severe skin reactions.
- **Health Hazards:** Some counterfeit products contain toxic chemicals that can lead to long-term health problems.

3. How to Ensure You Are Buying Original Products

Source from Authorized Distributors

One of the best ways to ensure you are buying original products is to source them from authorized distributors. Authorized distributors are officially recognized by the brands they represent and have a direct supply chain from the manufacturer to the retailer.

- **Verify Distributor Credentials:** Always check the credentials of your distributors. Authorized distributors should provide proof of their authorization from the brand.
- **Direct Communication:** Establish direct lines of communication with the brands you carry. This can help verify the authenticity of your suppliers.

Check Packaging and Product Details

Original products come with specific packaging and product details that are difficult to replicate. Pay close attention to these details when purchasing stock.

- **Packaging Quality:** Original products have high-quality packaging with clear printing, correct logos, and consistent colors. Counterfeit products often have packaging flaws.
- **Batch Numbers and Expiry Dates:** Check for batch numbers and expiry dates on the packaging. These should match the information provided by the brand.
- **Holograms and Seals:** Many brands use holograms, seals, or other security features to verify authenticity. Make sure these are present and intact.

4. Building Customer Trust with Original Products

Authenticity Matters

Be transparent with your customers about where you source your products. Display certifications or proof of authenticity from brands prominently in your store.

- **Proof of Purchase:** Keep receipts and invoices from your suppliers and make them available for customer verification if needed.
- **Brand Certification:** Display any brand certifications or awards that prove your commitment to selling genuine products.

Key Takeaways

Buy only original products; don't fall into the trap of purchasing duplicates.

Conclusion

In the world of beauty, trust is everything. Selling genuine products isn't just about avoiding legal trouble; it's a promise to your customers that you care about their well-being. By choosing authenticity, you're building a foundation of trust that goes beyond sales. It's about creating loyal customers who become brand advocates. Remember, your shop's reputation is like your skin – delicate and precious. Protect it by committing to genuine products and exceptional service.

Chapter 6

Make the Most of Company Offers

"The greatest glory in living lies not in never falling, but in rising every time we fall." – Nelson Mandela

The Importance of Utilizing Offers Provided by Companies

Running a successful cosmetic shop requires more than just stocking popular products and providing excellent customer service. One crucial aspect that can significantly impact your business's success is taking full advantage of the offers provided by cosmetic companies. These offers can include discounts, special promotions, bulk purchase deals, and more. This chapter will explain why it is essential to utilize these offers and how doing so can benefit your business.

1. Understanding Company Offers

Cosmetic companies frequently provide various offers to their retailers. These offers are designed to help shops like yours increase sales, attract more customers, and enhance profitability. Some common types of offers include:

- **Discounts on Bulk Purchases:** Companies may offer discounts when you purchase products in bulk. These discounts can significantly lower your costs and increase your profit margins.
- **Special Promotions:** These can include limited-time offers, holiday promotions, and new product launches. Participating in these promotions can attract customers looking for deals.
- **Free Sample:** Companies often provide free samples of new or popular products. These samples can be given to your customers as a way to encourage them to try and eventually buy the full-sized product.
- **Buy-One-Get-One-Free (BOGO) Offers:** These offers can help move inventory quickly and make room for new stock.
- **Exclusive Deals for Loyal Retailers:** Companies may offer special deals to retailers who consistently sell their products. These deals can include higher discounts, extended payment terms, and exclusive access to new products.

2. **Why Utilizing Company Offers is Essential?**

Increased Profit Margins

Taking advantage of bulk purchase discounts and other deals can significantly reduce your purchasing costs. Lower costs mean higher profit margins, allowing you to reinvest in your business, improve your store, or offer competitive pricing to your customers.

- **Cost Savings:** Bulk purchase discounts reduce the per-unit cost of products, increasing your overall profitability.
- **Higher Margins:** Selling products obtained at a discount at regular prices boosts your profit margins.

Moving Inventory Quickly

Utilizing offers such as BOGO can help you move inventory faster. This is particularly beneficial for seasonal items or products nearing their expiration dates.

- **Inventory Turnover:** Quickly moving inventory prevents stock from becoming outdated or expired, reducing waste and loss.
- **Fresh Stock:** Regularly refreshing stock keeps your store exciting for customers, encouraging them to return frequently.

Building Strong Relationships with Suppliers

Regularly participating in company offers can help build strong relationships with your suppliers. This can lead to additional benefits, such as exclusive deals, better terms, and priority access to new products.

- **Supplier Relationships:** Strong relationships with suppliers can lead to better terms and exclusive deals.
- **Priority Access:** Being a preferred retailer can provide you with early access to new and popular products.

3. How to Effectively Utilize Company Offers?

Stay Informed

To take full advantage of company offers, it's essential to stay informed about the latest promotions and discounts. Here are some ways to stay updated:

- **Regular Communication:** Maintain regular contact with your suppliers and company representatives. They can provide you with information about upcoming offers and promotions.
- **Newsletters and Emails:** Subscribe to newsletters and email updates from cosmetic companies. These communications often contain details about current and upcoming offers.
- **Industry Events:** Attend industry events, trade shows, and product launches. These events are excellent opportunities to learn about new products and promotions.

Plan Your Purchases

Careful planning is crucial to making the most of company offers. Consider the following tips:

- **Seasonal Planning:** Plan your purchases around seasonal trends. For example, stock up on popular summer products before the season starts, taking advantage of pre-season discounts.

- **Budgeting:** Allocate a portion of your budget specifically for taking advantage of company offers. This ensures you have the funds available when a good deal arises.

Key Takeaways

Don't miss out on the valuable offers provided by the company.

Conclusion

Think of company offers as free money for your business. By taking advantage of these deals, you're not just saving cash, you're also giving your customers more bang for their buck. It's a win-win! Smartly planned promotions can bring in new customers, keep old ones happy, and help you stand out from the crowd. Remember, it's not just about the discount; it's about building excitement and creating a buzz around your shop. So dive in, explore the offers, and watch your business flourish.

Chapter 7

Mastering the Art of Selling

"In sales, it's not about selling a product but about solving a problem." – Anonymous"

Latest Selling Techniques for Cosmetic Shop Owners

Selling cosmetics in today's market requires more than just stocking shelves with the latest products. It involves understanding customer needs, building trust, and utilizing modern selling techniques to make your suggestions relevant and persuasive. This chapter will explore the latest selling techniques, focusing on the belief that you can sell to customers and they will buy the products you suggest, as long as your suggestions match their reality.

Customer Profiling

Create detailed profiles of your typical customers. Consider factors such as age, gender, lifestyle, skin type, and beauty concerns. This information will help you understand what products are likely to appeal to them.

- **Age:** Younger customers might prefer trendy makeup, while older customers might be more interested in anti-aging products.
- **Gender:** While cosmetics are traditionally marketed towards women, there is a growing market for men's grooming products.
- **Lifestyle:** Busy professionals might prefer quick and easy-to-use products, while beauty enthusiasts might look for comprehensive skincare routines.
- **Skin Type:** Different skin types require different products. Knowing whether your customer has oily, dry, combination, or sensitive skin can guide your recommendations.
- **Beauty Concerns:** Addressing specific concerns like acne, dryness, or aging can make your suggestions more relevant and appealing.

Storytelling

Storytelling is a powerful way to connect with customers on an emotional level. Share stories about the products, the brand, or your personal experience with the products.

- **Brand Stories:** Share the story behind the brands you carry. This can include the brand's history, values, and what makes their products unique.
- **Personal Stories:** Share your own experiences with the products. Personal testimonials can be very convincing.

- **Customer Stories:** Highlight positive feedback and testimonials from other customers. This social proof can reassure new customers about the product's effectiveness.

Cross-Selling and Up-Selling

Cross-selling and up-selling can increase your sales and provide added value to customers.

- **Cross-Selling:** Recommend complementary products that enhance the effectiveness of the main product. For example, if a customer is buying a foundation, suggest a primer that helps the foundation last longer.
- **Up-Selling:** Suggest higher-end versions of the products they are considering. Explain the additional benefits and why it might be worth the extra cost.

Leveraging Technology

Utilizing technology can enhance the customer experience and streamline the sales process.

- **Point-of-Sale Systems:** Use modern point-of-sale systems to track sales, manage inventory, and gather customer data.
- **Customer Relationship Management (CRM):** Implement a CRM system to keep track of customer interactions and preferences. This can help you provide personalized service and follow-up.

Setting Realistic Expectations

Ensure that your recommendations set realistic expectations for the customer. Overpromising can lead to disappointment and loss of trust.

- **Benefits and Limitations:** Clearly explain the benefits of the product and any limitations. For example, a moisturizer might hydrate the skin but may not be effective for severe dryness.
- **Time Frame:** Set realistic expectations for how quickly the customer can expect to see results. Some products may take a few weeks to show noticeable effects.

Key Takeaways

Start believing that you can sell to customers and that they will buy the products you suggest, as long as your recommendations align with their needs and reality.

Conclusion

Mastering the latest selling techniques is essential for cosmetic shop owners who want to thrive in today's competitive market. By personalizing consultations, engaging through storytelling, strategically upselling and cross-selling, and making data-driven decisions, you can enhance your selling strategy and drive success in your business. Implement these techniques to create a compelling shopping experience that resonates with your customers and meets their needs, leading to increased sales and customer satisfaction.

Case Study: The Story of Gayatri Cosmetics

Gayatri opened a small cosmetic shop in her city. She knew that simply selling products wasn't enough; understanding her customers was crucial too. So, she decided to get to know her customers well.

Gayatri paid attention to her customers' age, gender, lifestyle, skin type, and beauty concerns. She discovered that young girls preferred trendy makeup products, while older women leaned towards anti-aging products. There was also a growing number of male customers who needed grooming products specifically for men.

Additionally, Gayatri considered her customers' lifestyles. Busy working women needed products that were quick and easy to use, while beauty enthusiasts wanted to follow a full skincare routine. Products also varied based on skin type. Gayatri tried to build a personal connection with her customers. She listened to them carefully and found solutions to their problems. She valued their stories and often shared her own experiences with the products she used.

In this way, Gayatri understood her customers well and tailored her shop to meet their needs. This not only increased her sales but also built trust with her customers.

Chapter 8

Direct Communication Tools for Your Cosmetic Shops

Connecting with Your Customers

In today's competitive market, staying connected with your customers is crucial for your cosmetic shop's success. Direct communication tools like WhatsApp, YouTube, Facebook, and Instagram Reels make it easy to engage with your customers in a personal and effective way. This chapter explains why these platforms are important and how they can help you build stronger customer relationships, increase engagement, and boost sales.

Why These Tools Are Important for Your Shop?

Direct communication platforms help you interact with customers more personally, allowing you to offer tailored advice and support:

- **WhatsApp:** With over 2 billion users globally, WhatsApp offers an intimate and immediate way to reach your customers. Its messaging service allows for personal, real-time communication, making it an excellent tool for customer support, sending product updates, latest schemes, and promoting special offers.

- **YouTube:** As the world's second-largest search engine, YouTube is a powerful tool for sharing video content that educates, entertains, and engages your audience. You can create video tutorials, product reviews, and behind-the-scenes content to showcase your cosmetic products and connect with viewers on a deeper level.
- **Facebook:** With its massive user base, Facebook is ideal for building a community around your brand. Utilize its messaging feature, Facebook Messenger, to offer personalized customer service, respond to inquiries, and share promotional content. Facebook's ability to create targeted ads and events also makes it a valuable tool for reaching a broader audience.
- **Instagram Reels:** Instagram Reels allows you to create short, engaging videos that can capture the attention of potential customers. By showcasing your products, beauty tips, schemes, and user-generated content, Reels can help increase your brand visibility and drive traffic to your shop.

How to Use These Tools Effectively?

To get the most out of these platforms, start by identifying where your customers are most active:

- **Create Engaging Content:** Share content that grabs attention, such as product launches, special offers, or beauty tips, tailored to each platform.
- **Personalize Your Messages:** Use customer names, reference past purchases, and offer recommendations to make your communication more personal.
- **Use Multimedia:** Incorporate images, videos, and voice messages to make your content more engaging and memorable.
- **Encourage Interaction:** Ask for feedback, run polls, and respond to customer questions to create a two-way conversation.

Best Practices

Respect Customer Privacy

- **Data Protection:** Ensure that customer data is protected and used responsibly. Follow data protection regulations and best practices across all platforms.
- **Opt-Out Options:** Provide easy ways for customers to opt out of receiving messages if they choose. Respect their preferences and promptly remove them from your list.

Maintain Professionalism

- **Clear and Concise Messages:** Keep your messages clear, concise, and relevant to the platform. Avoid overwhelming customers with lengthy or overly complex messages.

- **Proper Language:** Use appropriate grammar and spelling in your communications. Avoid slang or overly casual language, unless it aligns with your brand's voice.
- Brand Consistency: Ensure that your messages are consistent with your brand's voice and tone across all platforms. This helps reinforce your brand identity.

By using these direct communication tools, you can build stronger connections with your customers and keep them coming back to your shop.

Case Studies: Successful Use of WhatsApp in Cosmetic Shops

To illustrate the effectiveness of using WhatsApp for customer communication, here are a couple of case studies from cosmetic shops that have successfully implemented this strategy.

Case Study 1: Beauty Bliss

Beauty Bliss, a small cosmetic shop, wanted to increase customer engagement and drive more sales. They decided to use WhatsApp to achieve these goals.

By building a customer list, sending personalized messages, offering exclusive deals, and engaging with customers through interactive content, they boosted customer engagement and sales. WhatsApp's high open and response rates allowed Beauty

Bliss to build stronger relationships with their customers, leading to increased loyalty and repeat business. This case study demonstrates the potential of WhatsApp as a powerful marketing tool for small businesses.

Case Study 2: Glamour Glow

Glamour Glow, a mid-sized cosmetic retailer, wanted to improve customer experience and boost their marketing efforts using Instagram Reels.

By using Reels to announce new products, share beauty tips, and promote in-store events, they successfully increased event attendance and customer engagement. Instagram Reels allowed Glamour Glow to showcase their products in a fun and engaging way, helping them connect with customers on a deeper level and drive business growth.

Conclusion

Using direct communication tools like WhatsApp, YouTube, Facebook, and Instagram Reels can make a big difference for your cosmetic shop. These platforms help you connect with your customers in fun and personal ways, making them feel more valued and engaged. By sharing useful content, responding to questions quickly, and keeping your customers in the loop, you'll create a stronger bond with them. This connection will keep your customers coming back, helping your shop grow and succeed. Embrace these tools to create a buzz around your shop and watch your business grow!

Let's Conquer the Cosmetic Market

Thank you for taking the time to read this book. I hope the insights and strategies have sparked new ideas and enthusiasm in your journey. If you found value in these pages and are eager to dive even deeper into the world of cosmetic retail or have any questions, I'd love to hear from you. Your feedback is invaluable, and I'm here to continue the conversation.

Excited to take your ideas to the next level?

Have a vision you're passionate about? Let's talk! I'm excited to learn about your plans and see how we can achieve them together

Ashish Gupta

Cell +91 9560998866

Email Id:- Mail@indiahenna.com